Water

Water

Poetry by
Nima

Selected and adapted by
Abbas Kiarostami

A translation by
Iman Tavassoly and Paul Cronin

Sticking Place Books
New York

Dedicated by Abbas Kiarostami to
Cyrus Tahbaz

Shiva Sheybany
Sohrab Mahdavi
Stacey Knecht
and
Michael Beard
are thanked by the translators

© Sticking Place Books 2015

www.stickingplacebooks.com
www.lessonswithkiarostami.com
www.filmmakertrilogy.com

Design by Ryan Bojanovic

All rights reserved.
No part of this book may be reproduced, stored in or introduced into a retrieval system, or transmitted, in any form or by any means (electronic, mechanical, photocopying, recording or otherwise) without the written permission of the publishers, except in the case of brief quotations in critical articles or reviews.

ISBN 978-1-942782-16-2

Between 2006 and 2011, Iranian film director Abbas Kiarostami – author of three books of original verse – released his selections from and adaptations of four masters of Persian poetry: Nima (1895–1960), Hafez, Saadi and Rumi (all from the thirteenth and fourteenth centuries). This material is presented to English-speaking readers for the first time, in eight volumes: Hafez's *Wine*, Saadi's *Tears*, Nima's *Water* and Rumi's *Fire*. In 2015, Kiarostami published two further books, the thematic anthology *Night*, his selections from a variety of classical and contemporary poets, the English translation of which is issued in four volumes.

Kiarostami's project has been a contentious one, and in plucking fragments of poetry from longer works – an endeavour no less personal than the composition of original verse – he incurred the ire of critics in Iran. Some, whose lifelong pursuit has been the examination of the poets whose work Kiarostami presents in his volumes, believe him to be something of a dilettante, an interloper who lacks the skills required to handle this precious material. With no professional training in Persian literature, he is, they submit, unprepared for the task at hand, and some refuse to consider his work as legitimate poetry. In Iran, after all, poetry is treated with absolute seriousness, its authors regarded as the unveilers of vital secrets, endowed with powerful sensibilities, in effect keepers and revealers of the Persian soul. Certain books of verse are even treated as if they were holy texts, and it would not be unfair to suggest that the work of a handful of pivotal poets has profoundly influenced both the Persian language and, in turn, the daily lives of millions in modern Iran.

Still, along with criticism came praise. In publishing his straightforward selections for the general reader, it was noted that Kiarostami – whose work in any discipline attracts global attention – has opened up the world of Persian poetry to those largely unaware of this wondrous and vast body of work, especially readers beyond the borders of his homeland. "Some people, sitting at a dining table covered in fabulous food, don't know which dish to start with," says the meditative Kiarostami. These books are his way of navigating readers through that particular feast. Absorb and begin to understand these adaptations – "trailers," Kiarostami calls them – and we are, he believes, better equipped to tackle the originals in their fuller forms. There are many costly, ornate and ostentatious editions of poetry in Iran. But, says Kiarostami, such illuminated books exist "to be given as gifts, and rarely do they actually encourage reading." The opposite could be said of Kiarostami's versions: relatively inexpensive and unembellished, containing nothing but text. His self-professed and modest aim is to make an unequivocal and intimate connection between poem and reader, author and explorer.

So what precisely has Kiarostami done with the original texts? For his two *Night* volumes, he located lines of verse from an assortment of poets – venerable and present-day – each somehow relating to a single subject matter, and brought them together. ("It's worth noting," says Kiarostami, "that few of the poets write about what night actually is. Instead, the darkness and approaching dawn are used as reflections of feelings and inner conditions.") With all others, he has trimmed down poems by individual authors, pulled lines out of context and framed them piece by piece, at the same time retaining and thereby emphasising what he considers to be key concepts, characters and landscapes. Kiarostami has suggested that the unexpurgated originals are like crude oil, straight from the ground, in need of processing and refinement. By making his selections, deconstructing and breaking the metre of the original verse, cracking it open and removing the rhythm, Kiarostami has allowed specific ideas and themes to flow out in epigrammatic form. His reductionist method might be best understood by comparing a feature film, with its sweeping lines of narrative and interlocking characters, to a series of still photographs, each of which presents a single scene within a carefully constructed frame. It is as if Kiarostami has stood before a vast image, studied it carefully, isolated the elements he wants to accentuate, then affixed a frame over just one small part, so bringing to light something previously indistinct, almost unnoticeable, hitherto concealed.

Kiarostami's own poems are, more than anything, closest to Japanese Haiku, which is for the most part the form he has imposed upon his selections from the great masters. But in furnishing us with a mere three or four lines, Kiarostami – a practitioner of free verse, in both his adapted and original poetry – has striven to convey the essence, the fundamental meaning, of entire pages in the original. The result is a summary: poetry of minimalism. There is a startling compactness and simplicity to these books, with nothing extraneous, even if each page contains a discrete message and definite wisdom.

Kiarostami's process of creative condensation is uncomplicated and, to a large extent, intuitive. "In Paris one day I saw a book through a shop window," he explains. "On the cover was an enlargement of the corner of a Cezanne painting. It showed only an apple. The designer of the book cover hadn't negated the rest of the painting so much as magnified a piece of it, and by doing so asked the reader to explore this one piece of fruit. A poem is like wine, which should be enjoyed line by line, drop by drop. If you want to express love or hatred, or have been asked a question by someone, these books provide you with a great many potential responses. Younger readers will presumably appreciate their brevity, that they could be sent as graceful text messages. What's important is what the poet writes about. This is my priority, rather than how he tells it. I think more about effect than form. My duty is to transfer ideas to the audience. If this is best done in short bursts, if we are living in an age of concision, then so be it. It's important for me always to be experimenting, to re-think the kind of storytelling I involve myself with." Kiarostami explains little, instead pointing at what we should be looking at, proposing that we decipher things for ourselves. Almost every poem, however short, has more than one level of meaning and is therefore open to interpretation, although Kiarostami has suggested that the first message the reader arrives at is likely the one the poet, and Kiarostami himself, intended.

This is a body of work which for Kiarostami, who for decades had no intention of publishing his selections, has been a long time coming. "When I took Rumi's book in hand," he explains, "I realised that I had already done much of the required work because for twenty years I have been obsessively highlighting and isolating certain poems." At a Tehran event marking the publication of his Rumi volumes, Kiarostami offered a forthright explanation for his poetry project. "I hope you forgive my foolish courage. My aim with these books was never to integrate myself into the world of literature. This endeavour which I have undertaken – these selections, many of which are lesser-known verses – is not me meddling in your own work. I was consumed by literature and poetry long before I became a filmmaker." Whether or not the following are poems or aphorisms in disguise, this book – and every one of his published volumes of verse – represent deeply felt enthusiasms. As such, consider them an essential component of Kiarostami's oeuvre, one that includes films, photographs and installations. Put any number of his poems alongside, for example, *The Wind Will Carry Us*, or his still images of snowy landscapes, or "Forest Without Leaves," his three-dimensional art project consisting of hollow tubes, standing floor to ceiling, covered by life-size photographs of bark, and they take on an ever greater significance. The associations between all four forms of expression, the similarities in visual motifs and concepts, the common elements, the unity between settings, characters and themes all become quickly apparent. Whether using a camera, paintbrush, pen or (at home, quietly away from public view) wood chisel, Kiarostami's innermost preoccupations reveal themselves. Whichever vehicle he uses, again and again the same images and ideas are transported into the mind of the audience.

Chapter divisions in Kiarostami's Hafez book are his own, based on the subjects of the poems. Classical Persian poetry is traditionally arranged in reference to the final letter of each line. Kiarostami's original Saadi book is presented, chapter by chapter, in this way, but our translation is not (we have discarded all chapter divisions, while keeping the poems in exactly the same order). Kiarostami himself dropped from his Rumi book the traditional arrangement based on each line's final letter. In all of Kiarostami's adaptations, his alignment of poetry on the page is very much his own (including the layout, with one poem per page). While Hafez writes in the symmetrical ghazal form, Kiarostami breaks down this structure based on his own preferences. Likewise, where Kiarostami might use three lines, we use only two. The original Persian editions of these poems contain a number of errors, so in bringing these volumes to press we aim to present the most accurate versions of Kiarostami's adapted poetry available. There is occasional overlap between Kiarostami's single-author books and *Night*, with a small number of poems appearing in both.

As neither poets nor professional translators, we offer these fairly literal translations – something of a massive addendum to *Lessons with Kiarostami*, a book detailing Kiarostami's recognisably poetic approach to filmmaking, published simultaneously – at the very least so they may unveil some of the mainsprings of his work as a storyteller and creator of images, thereby offering insight into his work as a filmmaker.

Iman Tavassoly and Paul Cronin

You must be drawn to the past of man and you must search within it. You must sink into the grave of the dead, you must go to the solitary ruins and distant deserts and cry out, and you must also sit for long hours in silence. I say to you that if these do not exist, nothing exists.

Nima

I am like a river.
You can draw water
    from any part of me.

من به رودخانه شبیه هستم
که از هرکجای آن لازم باشد می توان آب برداشت.

I do not know to whom I should tell
the story of my suffering.

من ندانم
با که گویم شرحِ درد

While living and breathing I remain a servant to solitude.

بندهٔ تنهاییم
تا زنده ام

What can the afflicted do but accept?

مبتلا را چیست چاره
جز رضا؟

My heart is the message from beyond,
    where dreams and souls go to die.
Outwardly, it is the laughter of life.
All tears hidden within.

قلب من
نامهٔ آسمان هاست
مدفنِ آرزوها و جان هاست
ظاهرِش خنده های زمانه،
باطنِ آن
سرشک نهان هاست

I am in love, in love, in love.
Being in love is pain and sorrow.

عاشقم من
عاشقم من
عاشقم
عاشقی را
لازم آید
درد و غم

Movement of the sea, roaring waters.
Moonbeam.
Moonlight appears.
Rain falling, silence in the valleys.
The flight and wandering of moths.
The wailing of owls.
Darkness on the mount.
The weeping of a magnificent waterfall.
Birds calling, the sound of wings.
All this when I think of such things.

جنبشِ دریا، خروشِ آب ها
پرتو مه
طلعتِ مهتاب ها
ریزشِ باران، سکوتِ درّه ها
پرش و حیرانیِ شب پره ها
نالهٔ جغدان
و تاریکیِ کوه
های هایِ آبشارِ با شکوه
بانگِ مرغان و صدایِ بالشان
چون که می اندیشم از احوالشان

A small wooden hut near a place of ruin.
Do you remember?
An old woman of the village, spinning cotton, in tears.
Silence and darkness of night…
Outside rumbled cold winds.
Fire burning at the heart of the hut.
A girl – talking, wailing – bursts through the door.
"O my heart, my heart, my heart!"

در یکی کلبهٔ خُردِ چوبین
طرفِ ویرانه ای، یاد داری؟
که یکی پیرزنِ روستایی
پنبه می رشت و می کرد زاری
خاموشی بود و تاریکیِ شب…
بادِ سرد از برون نعره می زد
آتش اندر دلِ کلبه می سوخت
دختری ناگه از در در آمد
که همی گفت و بر سر همی کوفت
ای دلِ من، دلِ من، دلِ من!

Such flames that burnt through those dark nights!
Sheep and mountains nearby.
From time to time disturbance and commotion
    induced in the flock.
The call of shepherds.
The sound of murmuring.
The call of sheep bells.
The call of the flute.
City life abrades me.
City conversation torments me.

به به از آن آتشِ شب های تار
در کنارِ گوسفند و کوهسار!
به به از آن
شورش و آن همهمه
که بیفتد گاه گاهی در رمه
بانگِ چوپانان
صدای های های
بانگِ زنگِ گوسفندان
بانگِ نای!
زندگی در شهر فرساید مرا
صحبتِ شهری
بیازارد مرا

Separated from my origins, I have never been at peace.
I have become a seeker of suffering and adventure,
    quarrelling with my own evolution.
When it comes to life, I remain doubtful.
Now you, restless waves, take me, in sorrowful solitude,
    towards farthest hidden points.
It is here where those who have failed
    can retreat no more from salvation.

تا من از اصلِ خود
جدا شده ام
دمی آرامی ام نبوده به دهر
طالبِ رنج و ماجرا شده ام
کرده ام از شکفتنِ خود، قهر
مانده ام با زمانه در تردید
اینک ای موج های بی آرام!
ببریدم به سوی دورترین
نقطه های نهان که یک ناکام
بتواند در انزوای حزین
دورتر مانَد از
خلاصیِ خویش

I wish the soul had wisdom and intelligence.

کاش جان را
عقل بود و هوش بود

Simple thought.
Basic understanding.
Insignificant sorrow.

فکرِ ساده
درک کم، اندوهِ کم

Homeless am I in the sky.
This is hidden from the serene heart.
Lagging behind time and space.
Whatever I am, I am for lovers.
I am what you say.
I am what you want.

از دلِ بی هیاهو نهفته
من یک آوارهٔ آسمانم
وز زمان و زمین باز مانده
هر چه هستم
برِ عاشقانم:
آنچه گویی منم
و آنچه خواهی

O lover, arise!
Springtime!
A small spring welled up from the mountain.
Flowers on the plain resembling flames,
    dark river like sun storm.
Flowers have made colourful the plain.

عاشقا!
خیز که آمد بهاران
چشمهٔ کوچک از کوه جوشید
گل به صحرا، در آمد چو آتش
رودِ تیره
چو طوفان خورشید
دشت، از گل شده هفت رنگه

Who can love me and not selfishly profit by doing so?
Everyone races about for their own benefit.
No one picks a flower with no scent.
Love without enjoyment and benefit is a dream.

که تواند
مرا دوست دارد
و اندر آن بهرهٔ خود نجوید!
هر کس از بهر خود
در تکاپوست
کس نچیند گلی که
نبوید
عشق بی حظ و حاصل
خیالی است!

Everyone cast you away, not knowing you are eternal.
Who are you, cast away from every place?
Have you come here with me as would a friend?
Are you a teardrop?
Are you sorrow?

هر کس از جانبِ خود
تو را راند
بی خبر که تویی جاودانه
تو که ای
ای زِ هر جای رانده
با مَنَت بوده ره
دوستانه؟
قطرهٔ اشکی آیا تو
یا غم؟

Annihilator love.
I am love!

عشقِ فانی کننده
منم عشق!

I am the flower of love, born of tears!

من گلِ عشقم و
زادۀ اَشک!

The time of love and passion will pass.
Blaze of mind.
Blaze of soul.
Pain of separation.

بگذرد ایّام عشق و اشتیاق
سوزِ خاطر
سوزِ جان
دردِ فراق

The mass of snow split.
The mountaintop formed into two colours.
The shepherd emerged from the catacomb,
    laughing contentedly.
Time for grazing.

تودهٔ برف بشکافت از هم
قلّهٔ کوه شد یکسرِ ابلق
مردِ چوپان در آمد ز دخمه
خنده زد شادمان و موفّق
که دگر وقتِ سبزه چرانی است

Such a night!
Smiling moon.
Smooth grass.

چه شبی!
ماه خندان،
چمن نرم!

I am a lover, asleep and unaware.

عاشقم
خفته ام
غافلم من!

O my heart, my heart, my heart!
My poor, needy, worthy heart!
All your goodness, value and pride.
Yet what came of my time with you,
    save a tear upon the face of sorrow?

ای دلِ من
دلِ من، دلِ من
بی نوا، مضطر، قابلِ من!
با همه خوبی و قدر و دعوی
از تو آخر چه شد
حاصلِ من
جز سرشکی به رخسارهٔ غم؟

We could all be as obedient slaves,
    but love seeks flight at every moment.
It always notices the puzzles.
This conflict has embroiled us all.

می توان
چون غلامان، به طاعت
شنوا بود و فرمانبر، اما
عشق هر لحظه پرواز جوید
عشق هر روز
بیند معما
و آدمیزاده در این کشاکش

I am a lion, king of all animals, leader of the warrior army.
Since my mother bore me she has roared
    and taught me not to groan, but to roar.

منم شیر
سلطانِ جانوران
سرِ دفترِ خیلِ جنگ آوران
که تا مادرم در زمانه بزاد
بغرید و غریدنم یاد داد
نه نالیدنم

Me, fearless, when approaching the enemy.
My strong head and shoulders never bowed.
A benevolent mother raised me.
Out of wisdom, hoping for a courageous child,
    she kept me at a distance.

به وحشت بر خصم
ننهم قدم
نیاید مرا پشت و کوپال، خم
مرا مادر مهربان از خرد
چو می خواست بی باک بار آورد
ز خود دور ساخت

I prey upon things everywhere.
I sleep where I want.
My place of rest is any woodland.
I do not concern myself with poor and feeble tricksters.
Why should I worry?

مرا طعمه
هر جا که آید به دست
مرا خواب، آن جا که میلِ من است
پس آرامگاهم به هر بیشه ای
زکیدِ خسانم نه اندیشه ای
چه اندیشه ای است؟

Can you name the enemy that can challenge me?
What victory could ever slip through my fingers?
When the creator was bestowing traits
    he put victory into my paw and endowed me with dignity.

عدو کیست با من ستیزد همی؟
ظفر چیست
کز من گریزد همی؟
جهان آفرین چون بسی سهم داد
ظفر در سرِ پنجهٔ من نهاد
وزان شأن داد

I am in love with whatever moves.

من بر آن عاشقم که
رونده است!

My foot, tired.
In the desert.

پای من خسته
اندر بیابان

O beloved!
I have no idea how to respond to your letter.
You wrote poetry, I write poetry.
I think of you endlessly, either too little or too much.

مهربانا!
جوابِ کاغذ تو
من ندانم
چگونه باید داد!
شعر گفتی
به شعر می گویم
همه یادِ توام
چه کم چه زیاد

When was it that human beings
    perceived their immediate surroundings?
Whoever saw what was in the distance raced towards it.
Those who do not fully appreciate you
    are among your relatives and close acquaintances.

آدمی نزدیکِ خود را
کی شناخت؟
دور را بشناخت
سوی او بتاخت
آن که کمترِ
قدرِ تو داند دُرست
در میانِ خویش و
نزدیکانِ توست

O myth!
I do not want to be chosen and loved.
I was born up in the mountains, brought here by clouds.
Better to let me be in nature, in embrace of spring.

ای فسانه!
مرا آرزو نیست
که بچینندم و دوست دارند
زادهٔ کوه، آوردهٔ ابر
به که بر سبزه‌ام واگذارند
با بهاری که هستم در آغوش

My name will never be known throughout the world.
I will never be respected in any company.
Best that I avoid artless rascals.
I am better than them all.

نگردد در آفاق، نامم بلند
نگردم به هر جایگاه ارجمند
پس آن به مرا
چون از ایشان سرم
از این بی هنر رو بهان بگذرم
کشم پای پس

If you want to get on in the world, don't be so loathsome.

سود گِرت هست
گرانی مکن

Disengage from yourself for one single moment.

یک نفس از خویشتن
آزاد باش

The more people desire something,
    the more they are made ill and are slain.

طالبِ مطلوب
چو بسیار شد
چند تنی
کشته و بیمار شد

Is it fair that when a hungry lion is asleep
the fox gets whatever it wants?

روا باشد این که
شیری گرسنه
چو خسبیده است
بیاید به هر چیز، روباه دست؟

Lucky are those who do not know, who do not understand,
    who do not read.
They are people oblivious to all problems,
    unless those problems are their own.

ای خوشا آنان
که نمی دانند
که نمی فهمند، که نمی خوانند
که نمی جنبند، زابتلای خویش
جز برای خویش

Even when dust gets everywhere, when it falls upon the path before me, even upon me, my way is never lost.

گر از همه جا
غبار خیزد
بر راهِ من و به من بریزد
بر من نشود
طریقِ من گم

My straightness gives me strength.

وز راستی‌ام
مرا مدد هست

What should the poet do with his fear?

چه کند با هراس خود
شاعر؟

With every broken rule comes an opportunity
to find a path to life.

باهر خلاف
جستن راهی
به زندگی است

Many words were said, but many more are hidden.

بسیارها
سخن برفت و نهان تر
سخن بسی

When things are not working out, try as we might,
    should we not be more carefree?
If you are unable to win the fight, remove yourself from it.
If you cannot kill the snake on the road with your fist,
    do not kill yourself trying.

کار از جهدِ ما چو ناید راست
از خلاصی چرا بباید کاست
چو نداری مجال کین و ستیز
به که گیری از این میانه گریز
کشته ناید به ره چو مار به مشت
خویشتن بهرِ او نشاید کشت

Failure all over.
Everyone lacking dignity.
One person a success, yet still stripped of all dignity.

در این زمان
که هر کسی از پای می فتاد
از پا نمی فتاد
گر از جای می فتاد
چونان که آن دگر از پا فتادگان

Me, so heartbroken.
How sad that this heartbreak will fell me.

داغم من و
به حسرتم این داغ می کشد

Destruction of this garden kills twilight.

شبگیر را خرابی این باغ
می کشد

Three hundred and nine will pass before our mind's eye,
just as did three hundred and eight.

سیصد و نه
چنان که سیصد و هشت
خواهد از پیشِ ذهنِ ما بگذشت

Happy for what we have found,
   although still hidden from everyone.

گرچه شادان
که جمله یافته ایم
روی لکن ز جمله تافته ایم

Shame on us for not helping ourselves.

شرمی به روی ما
که ز خود دست بسته ایم

None but the dead have completely surrendered.

جز مُرده هیچ کس
تسلیمِ محض نیست

A horse arrives, separated from rider.

اسبی جدا ز صاحبش
از راه می رسد

Cold wind blew in from the mountain.

سرد بادی
دمید از برِ کوه

A branch from the roof, stripped, without leaves.

بی برگ و بی نوا
شاخی ز روی بام

Everyone told him not to go, but he chose not to listen.

همه گفتند مرو
او نشنید

My journey is not to my heart's content.
I need to journey to my heart's content.

به مرادم
نمی رود سفرم
سفری لازم است
سوی مراد

Although many searched and did not find,
 no one stopped searching.

گر چه بسیار کس
بجست و نیافت
کس نه از جست و جوی
روی بتافت

I am my only companion.

هیچ کس جز من
نباشد یارِ من

Unless old yourself, you cannot understand.
Elders' words are not those of youth.

پیر نا گشته ای، ندانی چیست
حرفِ پیرانه در جوانی نیست

There is no hesitation in the world.
This mirror will one day strike a stone.

نیست در عالم اجسام درنگ
خورَد این آینه یک روز
به سنگ

When destruction overwhelms your home,
   take it to the mountain.

چو خرابی گرفت خانهٔ تو
کوه بهتر
از آشیانه تو

Hope should be found in every dream.
All hopes began as dreams.

باید از هر خیال
امیدی جست
هر امیدی، خیال بود نخست

When willing to serve, one must free oneself from comfort.

گر به خدمت
کمر بباید بست
باید از یادِ راحتِ خود رست

In indigence is a man's brightness lost.

بی نوایی
جلایِ مرد بَرَد

Finding is the payoff of wanting.

یافتن
دستمزد خواستن است

Jobs are unobtainable and employers rare.

كار نایاب و
كار فرما كم

For results, go to the root of the lily.

بیخِ سوسن شو
از پیِ ثمری

Again and again the world opens and closes one curtain,
then shows its face from behind another.

چون جهان
پرده بس بست و گشود
وز دگر پرده نقش خود بنمود

Alive is the soul that arrives satisfied, then departs.
Dead is the soul that arrives covetous, then departs.

زنده جانی
که قانع آمد و شد
مرده آنی
که طامع آمد و شد

Why are you sitting in this cramped place?
Why not escape into the wide open?
For how long will you sit inside this cage,
    suffering and singing in remembrance of springtime?
For how long will you be like Harut,
    down in the bottom of the well?
If you are a miraculous moon, come shine upon us.
No cloud ever settled in one place.
No bird ever nested in a single spot.
Why close the door to contemplation?
It is like sitting at home in a grave.

چه نشینی
در این نشیمنِ تنگ
نگریزی چرا به صد فرسنگ؟
در قفس چند خواندن
از سرِ درد
یادِ روزِ بهار و موسمِ ورد؟
همچو هاروت
تا به کی در چاه؟
گر مهِ نخشبی برآی به راه
ابر یک جای بین
که خانه نکرد
بر یکی شاخ، مرغ لانه نکرد
راهِ نظاره را چرا بستن
چو بگوری به خانه بنشستن

O it is said that when one day passes,
    all things will pass with that day!
It is said that life is but a dream,
    that one should not bother one's mind about it.
But this is all nonsense.
Nothing passes in front of my eyes without burning.
I draw its image.
I remember everything.

آه! می گویند
چون بگذشت روزی
بگذرد هر چیز با آن روز
باز می گویند خوابی هست
کارِ زندگانی
زآن نباید یاد کردن
خاطرِ خود را
بی سبب نا شاد کردن
بر خلافِ یاوهٔ مردم
پیشِ چشمِ من ولیکن نگذرد
چیزی بدونِ سوز
می کشم تصویرِ آن را
یادِ من می آید
از آن روز!

How can you be so ambitious on this narrow path,
    where so many tears are shed?
You there!
Free yourself from ambitious dreams.
Lighten the load.
Calm yourself.

در چنین تنگ راه شیون ساز
دل چه داری در آرزوی دراز؟
هان از این خواب های سودایی
سبکی گیر تا بیاسایی

I take no benefit from her kindness.
Why am I so pained by the wound she caused?

چو
نه از مهرِ او مرا
سود است
زخم او خوردنم چه مقصود است؟

A man never breaks his promise.

نگسلد مرد
چون کند پیمان

Every pattern, thanks to the delicate touch of the pen.

همه این نقش‌ها که در رقم است
از سبکبار رفتنِ قلم است

Since learning the language of night,
    my heart has understood the reasons for many things.
Heart darkened, hair whitened.
From dark clouds above, water rained upon the farm.
A pen the colour of night writes brightly.
A pattern appears from the darkness.
Contemplating this all night,
    by morning the key had dropped into my lap.

تا دل من زبانِ شب دانست
از بسی چیزها سبب دانست
دل سیه شد که موی کرد سپید
آب، ز ابرِ سیه به کشت رسید
قلم از رنگِ شب به سامان شد
رقم از تیرگی نمایان شد
چو نمایان شدم بدین امید
صبح را برِ کفم فتاد کلید

If you arrive at a mirage instead of water,
    be thirsty and cherish the moment.
Embrace life as I do.
If life offers you a drink of bitterness, taste it.
What could be more inspiring
    than drinking from the cup of life?
Why all these complaints when life is going so well?
Why all these tears?

به سرابی اگر آمدی نه بر آب
تشنه می مان و وقت را دریاب
همچو من روزگار در بر کش
شربتِ زهر اگر دهد می چش
شربت از دست او چو می نوشی
چه تو را طامعی کر آن جوشی
روزگارت چو روزگار بداد
چیستت بر لب، از چه رو فریاد؟

Let no one in.
Separate yourself from good and bad
    if you are not party to this corruption.

خلوت آور
جدا ز هر بد و نیک
نیستی گر در این فساد شریک

Be like a river, moving through life.
Sometimes raging, sometimes at a standstill.

در مثل رود باش، از پیِ زیست
هم شتاب آورد به راه،
هم ایست

The ultimate desire of fruit is to ripen.

ذوقِ هر میوه
در رسیدن اوست

Old wheat is better than fresh barley.

گندم کهنه
به ز تازه جوی

Life itself is an indication of will.

زندگی
خود نشانِ خواستن است

Years of suffering have seasoned me.

سال‌ها درد
پرورانده مرا

Although you guard treasure, you have no treasure,
while I, with my ailments, at least have pain.

تو به گنجوریت اگر بی گنج
من ز رنجوریم، نیم بی رنج

I wish I had not spoken to her.
By doing so I broke her heart.

کاش با او نگفتمی سخنی
تا نبودش به دل ز من شکنی

I emerge from my corner, finding reason to push on.
I stand, once again facing the desert,
    as powerful as when I began.

پای از گوشه ای بر آوردم
رغبتِ راه در سر آوردم
روی دارم سوی بیابان باز
زان سبک تر که
بودم از آغاز

Hey caged bird!
Where do you imagine yourself?
On which box tree branch?
The city of happiness, with all its sparkle, is cracked.

ای مرغ در قفس!
ز کجا یاد می کنی
یاد از کدام شاخهٔ شمشاد می کنی؟
شهرِ طرب گسست
هر جلوه اش که بود

Remove yourself from the dark house of imagination
   towards your true path.

از سیه خانهٔ خیال
برآی
سوی راهی که راهِ توست
درآی

Although many words were spoken, better not to speak.
The best words are of the path.

گر چه
بس حرف رفت و کوته به
از همه حرف
حرف از ره به

In this house I play a guest.

من در این خانه
جای مهمانم

Although you are unable to touch her,
 why not at least take a first step?

دست اگر سوی او فرا نرسد
پای بر کوی او چرا نرسد؟

Innocents are not born of dust and water.
A true sinner will eventually self-destruct.

آن که نآلوده دامن از پاکی
نیست مولودِ آبی و خاکی
آنچه آب و گلش بینگیزد
لاجرم گنده از تنش خیزد

O better to stop speaking,
    for speaking is the curse of the soul!
The truth is that language is a curse.

حرف ای بس که
آمد آفتِ جان
راست گفتند
آفت است زبان

So long as there is hope, no heart is free.

تا امیدی است
رسته نیست دلی

Too much treasure and too many treasure maps.

گنج بسیار و
گنج نامه بسی

The beloved was nourished by me.
Then she departed.

دوست
گرمی ز من گرفت و
برفت

So many pointless treasure seekers.
Treasure fills their pockets, but still they search.

ای بسا گنج خواهِ بیهده سنج
گنج در جیب و
او به جستن گنج

Amid the bewilderment of a mind maze
    we search for a shadow.
There is nothing more.

در مکافاتِ فکرِ پیچاپیچ
در پیِ سایه ایم و باقی هیچ

The storyteller left.
His story remained.

قصّه گو رفت و
قصّه او ماند

Of conflicts around the world, one strikes your eye
 and one hundred strike the soul.

فتنه ها
کاندر این جهان خیزد
یک به چشم و صدش به
جان خیزد

She led me from the path and I followed.
Had I not been misled, I would be free.

ز راهم برد
و آنگاهم به ره کرد
گر از ره می نرفتم
می رهیدم

"No one will see my house," someone once said,
    "although my door is open to people unknown.
Better to drive visitors away than host unwanted guests."

گفت:
«هرگز کس نبیند خانه‌ام را
بر رخ هر ناشناسی در گشوده
میهمانَ راندن بسی خوش‌تر
که بَد را میزبان گشتن»

Even if I wear just one article of clothing
    from the thousand you have given,
        there can be no doubt of your generosity.
If I am miscast in this story, search only for meaning.
The story is merely words on a page.

گر بپوشیدم از هزار یکی
در هزارت مباد هیچ شکی
ور در اندامِ قصّه ام نه درست
قصّه، حرف است
نکته باید جست

My heart and the hope that nourishes.

دل ما بود و
امیدِ دلجو

This is a human being en route.

این آدمی بوَد
به رهی

How foolish to give up on treasure
    because of the troubles involved in finding it.

ابلهی باشد
زِ گنجی بگذری
از بیمِ رنج

Is it for our pleasure that the bird on the cypress branch sings so beautifully?

خوشنوایی که به شاخِ سرو می خواند
بهرِ لذّت بردنِ ما هست آیا؟

Keep your body in prison.
Release your mind from prison.

جسم
در زندان بدار و
فکر
از زندان برآر

The curtain is a barrier.
You can be one person in front, another behind.

پرده یعنی
پیشِ روی خود بداری حایلی
در پسِ پرده دگر باشی و
پیشِ آن دگر

A bird sits on the roof of our house,
    singing a faint and strange story.
Uncaged and free, still it sings a story for us.

مرغی نهفته
بر سرِ بام سرای ما
مبهم حکایتِ عجبی ساز می دهد
از ما برستهای است
ولی در هوای ما
بر ما، در این حکایت
آواز می دهد

Of the dervish nothing remained.
Neither wife nor child, nothing more, nothing less.
Yet how good to remember him.
He reached the end of the path.
He brought the story to an end.

گر چه
بر جا نماند از آن درویش
زن و فرزند و از کم و از بیش
یاد بادش که
ره به پایان بُرد
قصّه ای را چنین
به سامان برد

Alas!
Where in this dark night can I hang my tattered gown
    and so remove the arrows from my injured heart?
Alas!

وای بر من!
به کجای این شب تیره بیاویزم
قبای ژنده خود را
تا کشم از سینهٔ پر دردِ خود بیرون
تیرهای زهرِ را دلخون؟
وای بر من!

Be straight as a flower and carry a weapon.
On this path wear thorns upon your head.
Even if a flower has one hundred thorns,
    its value is undiminished.

راست چون گل،
سلاح در بر باش
اندر این راه
خار بر سر باش
گل اگر صد سلاح دارد راست
رونقِ روی او نخواهد کاست

I wish he could come through this window.
I would call him from afar.
"Come!"
"Woman," I would tell Aliyeh, my wife,
    "my father has come, so open the door."

کاش می آمد
از این پنجره، من
بانگ می دادمش از دور:
بیا!
با زنم عالیه، می گفتم: زن!
پدرم آمده
در را بگشا!

In the city of the blind my vision troubles me.
How futile it would be to blow a horn and announce my arrival.
Such childish behaviour that would be.

در درونِ شهرِ کوران
دردها دارم ز بینایی
همچنین هرگز نخواهم در میانِ بوق
بیهوده دمیدن،
تا بدانندم کسان اکنون رسیده ستم
این شتابِ خام زیبد
کودکان را

Should life be unsullied, free of mendacity?

زندگانی
بی دروغ و کاست باید باشد آیا!

Do not abandon me, helpless, weeping, in this rain.

زیرِ بارانم
زار و نالان اینچنین مگذار!

Life is the darkness of night and morning light.
A different manifestation in every direction.
What, then, at the end?
What rider can tame this wild horse?

زندگانی تیره ای هست از شبی و
روشنی از صبح فامی
جلوه ای هرگونه اش از گونه ای دیگر
چه ولیکن در سرانجام؟
تیزپای سرکشِ این زندگی را
کو سواری تا بدارد آرام؟

Victory belongs not to winners but to the free,
  even those behind walls.

فتح
مالِ آن کسانی نیست
که اکنون فاتح اند
فتح
مالِ مردمِ آزاده است
ار چه به بند.

Night hides our imperfections, as it does our strengths.

شب به معنی
عیب‌پوشِ مردمان است
آنچنانی که هنرها نیز
اندر او نهان است

I escape what once I chased.
I have reached the point where I battle against myself.

ز آنچه روزی در پی اش می رفتم
اکنون می گریزم
من بدان حالت رسیده ستم که
با خود می ستیزم

I have been friendly with poets since childhood.

من ز وقتِ کودکی
شاعران را
دوست بودم

Did not those who broke their promise
  come together once again?

آنان که
نشانِ عهدِ خود بشکستند
آیا نه دگر باره به هم پیوستند

I am an honourable neighbour
    from the slopes of nearby beautiful mountains.
Do our cows not graze together?
In spring we milk them side by side.

من یکی از
آبرومندان و از همسایگان هستم
در نشیبِ کوه های با صفا
نه دور پرِ زین جا
گاوهای ما مگر با هم ناستادند
در یک جا
ما به یک جا شیرِمان را در بهار
اندازه می گیریم

All day beneath the green willow tree he sat, head bowed,
    like the branches of the willow.
His grief caused by heart-rending love.
Everyone heard his tears.
O cheerless lover!
Sing beneath the green willow!

بر پای بیدِ سبز
نشسته تمام روز
افکنده سر فرود، چنان شاخه های بید
بود از برای عشق دلازار خود به سوز
هر کس صدای گریه اش
از دور می شنید
ای عاشقِ فسرده
بخوان زیرِ بیدِ سبز!

Whoever battles against evil is entwined with evil.
This is an ancient ritual, part and parcel of life.
Such deceitful people!
O meaningless life!
O futile life!

با بدان هر کس که بستیزد
بیش تر با هر بد آمیزد
این کهن رسمی است ما را
در نهادِ زندگی
چه مزوّر مردمانی!
آه یاوه زندگانی!
آه! ناقص زندگانی!

If we enter hurriedly through one door, we depart,
    unhappy, through another.
When the heart is consumed with profit and loss,
    life drains out.

از دری آمدیم گر
به شتاب
بر شدیم از در دگر
به خراب
دل که در کار سود
یا ضر شد
عمر بود الغرض که بر سر شد

Truly beautiful is life in mountains and villages.
Yet a day will come when humans are powerless,
    when the beauty of nature appears as but a scourge.
There can be no remedy for his pain.

راست می باشد که
کوه و زندگانی در دهستان
دلکش و زیباست
لیک روزی می رسد
که آدمیزاده نوایی نیستش
دلکشی های طبیعت
جز بلایی نیستش
و نخواهد بود درمان از پیِ رنجش!

My farm dried up.
All solutions proved useless.
The enemy, so cunning, has discovered my weakness.
Alas!
He prepares to shoot arrows tipped with hatred
    into my heart.

كشتگاهم خشک ماند و
یکسره تدبیرها
گشت بی سود و ثمر
تنگنای خانه ام را یافت
دشمن با نگاهِ حیله اندوزش
وای بر من!
می کند آماده بهرِ سینهٔ من
تیرهایی که به زهرِ کینه آلوده ست

In our mountains is a bird that sings atop silent lonely rocks.
It knows no language but its own.

در کُهستان های ما
مرغی است که
به روی صخره های خلوت و خاموش
می خواند
او زبانی جز زبان خود نمی داند

Poetry is important.
The poetic life is one of the richest to be had.
Whoever walks this path never searches in vain.

شعر را
رتبت بسی بالاست
زندگیِ شاعرانه با نواتِ زندگانی های این دنیاست
آن که در این راه می پوید
خیره چیزی را نمی جوید

There is madness in my nature.
If people are not at rest, I cannot be at rest.
If one day I weep because I have no bread,
    it is because I cannot give life to others.

در نهادِ من جنونی هست، که
اگر مردم نیاساید
من ندانم راهِ آسودن
من اگر روزی بنالیدم
ز بی نانی
بوده است از بهرِ یک دم
زندگانی

For a moment my acquaintances are near enough to talk to.
Because I cannot place fire in their hearts and none of them
understand my words, they walk away.

آشنایانم به صحبت با من
از یک دم شده نزدیک
چون در ایشان آتشِ من در نمی گیرد
و یکی نتواند از ایشان
حرفِ من که آید مرا
از دل به گوشِ دلش بپذیرد
دوری از من می گزینند

Is it really true that life is free of corruption?
The end of this night is nothing but the light of bright day.

این راست است
زندگی این سان پلید نیست؛
پایانِ این شب
چیزی به غیرِ روشنِ روزِ سفید نیست

I light my candle in darkness so that if I again collapse
I can burn in my tears.

شمع خود را من
درون تیرگی هایی می افروزم
که گر از پای در آیم باز
بتوانم دمی در اشکِ خود سوزم

The fabric of my life, woven from regrets.
Alas!
I fear that humans, tiring of what they have in hand,
   constantly reach for things beyond.

از بسی حسرت سرشتِ من سرشته ست
ای دریغا من
می اندیشم که آدمی سیری پذیر است از
هر آن چیزی که در کف دارد آن را
و مدام اندر تلاشِ دست یابیدن
بدان چیزی است کز او دور است

There is a connection between the faces and nature
 of evil people.
In darkness of night they appear as the sum total
 of the world's ugliness.

هست پیوندی میان روی و
خویِ مردمِ دد
خوب می بینم در این تاریکیِ شب
مثل اینکه
حاصلِ جمع اند آنان
جملهٔ زشتی های گیتی را!

Friendship and enmity are actually the same thing.

دوستی و دشمنی مردمان
- گر راست خواهی -
هر دو یکسان است

Whatever is designed to grow will grow because of clouds.

آنچه می باید روید، روید
از نمِ ابری
اگر چه سیراب

Searching, growing, gushing.
The heart.

می کاود و
می روید و
می جوشد
دل

Deserving of a father like me is a son like you.

در خور همچو
منی
پسرِ همچو
تویی

Tuberose under dew.

گل مریم
به زیرِ شبنم ها

After coldness of winter days come days of spring.

از پسِ سردیِ روزانِ زمستان است
روزانِ بهاری

If bitterly I sit on silent lips, if regrettably I add to or
    relieve suffering, I am the smile of bitter and painful days.
Me, the lone lover.

گر به تلخی
بر لبِ خاموش واری می نشینم،
گر به حسرت
می فزایم، یا به رنجی می گشایم،
من، من لبخندهٔ روزانِ تلخ و دردناک،
بی دلی خلوت گزینم

O meaningless life!
In the springtime of her laughter
    the newly blossomed flower passes away.
Pleasant morning lives for only a moment.
Human beings, alone with their pain.

آه! یاوه زندگانی!
در بهارِ خنده هایش نوشکفته گل بمیرد
صبحگه با آن صفای خود
یک دم افزون تر نپاید!
آدمی تنهاست
با دردی که دارد

Two years have passed since his sad loss.
Autumn leaves, twice upon his grave.
Three weeping broken shadows
    hanging from the branches of another shadow.

دو سال از نبودِ غم انگیزِ او گذشت
روی مزارِ او
دو بار برگ های خزان ریخته شدند
سه سایهٔ شکستهٔ گریان
بر شاخه های سایهٔ دیگر
آویخته شدند

O you, sitting upon the seashore, happy and laughing!
Someone is dying in that water.
There is always someone that you know
    struggling in this angry, dark, solemn sea.

آی آدم‌ها که بر ساحل نشسته
شاد و خندانید!
یک نفر در آب دارد می سپارد جان
یک نفر دارد که دست و پایِ دائم می زند
روی این دریای تند و تیره و سنگین
که می دانید

This time, his wing deep in blood.
The owl, silent, sitting on the stone.

این زمان بالَش
در خونش فرو
جغد
بر سنگ نشسته است
خموش

With so much hidden pain, it became clear to me:
Much suffering must be endured when courting the beloved.
Many untrodden paths must be walked.

با جهانی درد پنهان، بود این نکته به من معلوم
کز پی دیدارِ جانان
رنج ها بایست بگزیدن
بس رهِ نارفته می باید بریدن

If you have day, you will have night.

روزی ار باشد،
شبی دارید

So long as I live will my ignorance bring me suffering.

زنده‌ام تا من
مرا بوجهلِ من، در رنج دارد

Here I sit, having fled dark weather – with its polluted heart,
   its cold breeze – and your poisonous breath.
Allowing my heart to be trapped in this quiet corner,
   my path leads away from your poisonous breath.
Wherever you are, hidden from people, there I am.

من در اینجایم نشسته
از دلِ چرکین دمِ سردِ هوای تیره
با زهرِ نفس هاتان رمیده
دل به طرفِ گوشه ای خاموش
بسته
راه برده پس برون تیرگی های نفس های
به زهر آلودتان در هر کجا
هر سو که نهان هستید از مردم
منم حاضر

O you, welcome to the anguished hideaway
    of a wandering poet!
Bring that backpack filled with my poems
    so I might place it under my head.
I find myself beneath the sheltering sky,
    my feet far from familiar terrain.
No matter if my grief diminishes or not.
My deep sleep ravaged, as I intended.

ای که در خلوتِ سرای
دربارِ شاعرِی سرگشته داری جا
کوله بارِ شعرهایم را بیاور
تا به زیرِ سر نهاده
- رویِ زیرِ آسمان و پای دورم
از دیاران -
از غم من گر بکاهد یا نکاهد
خواب سنگینم رباید
آنچنان که دلم خواهد

At every turn I fear that nothing but a sigh
 will remain of me.

هرِ زمان
اندیشم از من در جهان
چیزی نماند
غیرِ آهی

Time for the king of kings to meet a shepherd
 who hails from villagers.

نوبت دیدار آمد
شهریارِ شهریاران را
با یکی چوپان
از شکفته دودمانِ روستایان

I will never forget that sweet moment,
    on the slope of dark valleys.
A cloud was on its way to meet the early morning moment.
Movement in all that was silent.
Shepherds herding flocks with serene songs
    from tambourine and flute.

هیچ وقتم آن دمِ شیرین نخواهد شد فراموش
در نشیبِ درّه ها تاریک زابری که به استقبالِ
وقتِ صبحدم می رفت
بود جنبیدن
هر چه را خاموش خاموش
و به نغمه های آرامِ دف و نی
گله می رانند چوپانان

Dear friend!
Cherish the time you have with the beloved.
If in that lonely place you find a heart loyal and sympathetic,
  never peddle those moments to the unkempt.

ای رفیق من! غنیمت دان
دمی گر صحبتِ جانانِ تو را
میسور افتاد
اندر آن خلوت
دلی گر محرم و همدرد می یابی
نوبتِ صحبت
به هیچ آلوده ای مفروش

Nothing happens in the heart of a simple and silent hut.
But there is news.

در دلِ کومهٔ خاموش فقیر
خبری نیست، ولی هست خبر

With each delay comes much good news.

در هرِ درنگ که باید
بسیار مژده هاست

Amid turmoil of endless suffering
are qualities of men revealed.

آید اندر کشمکشِ رنجِ مدید
ارزشِ مرد پدید

The night is long, the desert dark.

شب دراز است و
بیابان تاریک

I want no one to see me and want to see no one.
In the passion of my unquestioning contemplation,
    amid hordes of myriad agonies,
        the pain in my bones will do.

من نمی خواهم
کسم ببیند، یا ببینم کس
در تمنّای نگاهِ بی سؤالم
و ردیفِ رنج های بیشمارِ من
دردهای استخوانم بس

You seek war so as to benefit from antagonisms
    stirred up among everyone.

جنگ را تنها تو
از بهرِ به هم بد کردنِ مخلوق
می خواهی
تا توانی از رهِ آن
سودِ خود جویی

Life is nothing but a hustle, so stop worrying.
Whenever things are tough, be more carefree.

زندگی چون نبود
جز تک و تاز
خاطر این گونه
فرسوده مساز!
بگذران سهل در آن دم که به ناچار تو را
کار آید دشوار

Every step is afraid of the next.
A naked man, hand in hand with orphan child,
    en route to the village.
Shhh!
Dark night endures.

قدم از هر قدمی
دارد بیم
به رهِ دهکده مردی عریان
دست در دستِ یکی طفل یتیم
هیس!
آهسته شبِ تیره هنوز

Ding-dong!
It is within the meditation of life.
It is the path to the day of deliverance.
The key to morning appears with it.
Dark night ends with it.

دینگ دانگ!
در مراقبهٔ زندگی که هست
این هست ره به روزِ رهایی
با اوکلیدِ صبح نمایان
از او شبِ سیاه به پایان

Ding-dong!
What's that noise?
A bell!
Who died?
Who still breathes?

دینگ دانگ!
چه صداست؟
ناقوس!
کی مرده؟
کی به جاست؟

Many times, like dancing shadows on water,
    have one thousand experiences been unleashed.
Yet the sleeper never once awoke.

بس وقت شد
چو سایه که بر آب
وز او هزار حادثه بگسست
وین خفته برنکرد سر از خواب

Ding-dong!
Every breath offers a path to life, from dawn of existence to dawn of nothingness.

دینگ دانگ! ...... دم به دم
راهی به زندگی است
از مطلعِ وجود
تا مطرحِ عدم

Passion for the race.
Escaping the bad.
Engaging with good.

سودای تاختن
از بد گریختن
با خوب ساختن

The secret is revealed!
Things change.

این نکته گشته فاش
کاین کهنه دستگاه
تغییر می کند

Hand in hand with the one you know.
Shroud yourself in happiness and joy.
Listen to a love poem.
Praise her beauty mark.
Spend a night not thinking about
    what does and does not exist.

دست در دستِ کسی کآن دانید
خوش و خوشحال بپوشید شما
غزلی بشنوید
وصفِ خالی و لبی
بی خیال
از همه هست، از همه نیست
بگذرانید شبی

Unless the rust of an empty mind is eliminated from the heart,
    we are undeserving of desire.
Ha!
No door is opened before our eyes without purpose.

تا آدمی ز دل نزداید
زنگِ خیالِ پوچ
شایستهٔ نیاز نگردد
هیهات!
هیچ در
به رخ ما
بیهوده باز نگردد

Keep your window open before my eyes.
My heart longs to be with you for a moment.
I have it in my heart to sing for you.

به رویم پنجره ات را باز بگذار!
به دل دارم دمی
با تو بمانم
به دل دارم
برای تو بخوانم

Why close our eyes to this lively world?
Whoever has known no beauty in his life
　himself boasts no beauty.

دلگشا هست جهان
چشم چرا بستن از آن؟
آن که نشناخته در زندگی اش زیبایی
نیست زیبایی
در هیچ کجاش

I stretched out my hands, near and far,
   towards the joyful musicians of the wind.
They brought a message from the newly blossomed spring.
To break the bitter silence of the valleys I asked for help
   from those whose heart-warming music brings rapture
   and adds intensity to joy.

دست یازیدم
سوی آهنگ پردازانِ خرّمِ بادها
دور و نزدیک
که از بهارِ نوشکفته بودشان پیغام
از کسانی که شعف
از دلگشای آهنگشان خیزد
و به شدّت های شادی ها می افزاید
مدد جستم
تا سکوتِ تلخ را در درّه ها
دیوار بشکافم

Shame on me, miserable me!
In the heart of this dark night, who watches over me?
What can remedy this?
O God!
What brought me to this tearaway sea
    with hands empty of daily bread?
The beams of what longing have brought me here?
From weary seashore afar comes no burning light.

وای من، بر من زار!
در دلِ این شب تاریک
نگهبانم کیست؟
آنچه درمانِ مرا دارد
در کارم چیست؟
با کفم خالی از رزق- خدایا!- چه مرا
سوی این سرکش دریا آورد؟
روشنای چه امیدیم در اینجا ره داد؟
بر سرِ ساحل وامانده نمی سوزد، دلمرده چراغی
هم اکنون از دور

I should walk my path.
No one will care for me.
Although they would deny it, in this bustle of life,
    everyone is actually lonely.
My work protects me.

من به راهِ خود
باید بروم
کس نه تیمارِ مرا خواهد داشت
در پیِ از کشمکشِ این زندگیِ حادثه بار
- گرچه گویند نه -
هر کس تنهاست
آن که می دارد تیمار مرا
کارِ من است

I am innocent.
Fishing is my work, hoping for daily bread.
My life has gone to waste.
No one in this world, this world in which we live
    with bloody hearts, can be more impoverished than me.

بی گناه هستم من
کارِ من صید در آب
وندر امیدِ چه رزقی ناچیز
همه عمرم به هدر رفته
برِ آب
تنگ روزی تر از من کس نیست
در جهانی که
به خونِ دلِ خود باید زیست

Hands move upon the crest of waves.
Naked bodies – dancing and flowing – entwined.

بر سریرِ امواج
دست ها می گذرند
برهنه پیکرگانی در هم
رقص برداشته، ره می سپرند

Tide upon tide.
High to low, low to high.
The sea at work.

موج می خاست ز موج
از فرازی سوی زیر
از رهِ زیر به رو
بود دریا در کار

I was received into the circle of love.
A pity that my weary heart isn't also rested.
The flood of tears carries me along.
The homesick heart envelops.
What if my path leads not to the home of the beloved?

من که
در دایرهٔ عشقم سامان دادند
حیف باشد که
دلِ خسته به سامان نبرم
می برد سیلِ سرشکم به هوایِ دلِ تنگ
وای اگر
راه به منزلگهِ جانان نبرم!

Where should I go?
Who should I be thinking about?
You, my eyeliner, are at this moment my cure-all.
I shall not stop loving you.

به کجا راه برم؟
به چه کس در نگرم؟
توتیای چشمم
نوشداروی من این لحظه
تویی
بر نمی دارم من مهر از
تو

Why such pretense?
Even if life isn't about the search, it must still be lived.

وانمودی به چنین شیوه که هست
از پی چیست؟
از پی خواستنی نیست اگر
که آدمیزاد به ناچارش می باید زیست

Hey Rana! Rana!
Your body like a gazelle, Rana!
Magic-eyed Rana!
Hey Rana! Rana!

آی رعنا، رعنا!
تنِ آهو رعنا!
چشم جادو رعنا!
آی رعنا، رعنا!

A neighbour is a companion of a neighbour.

هست همسایه
به همسایه قرین!

Empty house.
Ecstatic guard.

خانه خالی است
نگهبان سرمست

Moon emerging, concealed by cloud.

ماه در ابر
نهان می‌آمد

Late stepped the man from the path.
He arrived by morning.

مردِ دیر آمده از راهِ سفر
صبح رسید

You may know how painful is the moment.
A human being understands but is unable to express things,
    as do poets, in words.
My heart, filled with grief.
I am in the same boat.
I appreciate the sorrow of the poems of the poets.

گر بدانی چه ملامت آور است آن دم
که آدمی می فهمد امّا آن توانایی نیستش
تا همچنان که شاعران
مقصودِ خود را بر زبان آرد
از همین ره بس مرا غم هاست
اندر دل
من غم انگیزیِ شعرِ شاعران را
دوست می دارم

No one sees the end of these days.
No one knows how far these wings will fly, to what land.
They are all blind.
Suddenly, something startling!
The wrong man, energetic, rises.
The wise man, dispirited, sits.

هیچ کس پایانِ این روزان نمی داند
بُردِ پروازِ کدامین بال
تا سوی کجا باشد
کس نمی بیند
ناگهان هولی برانگیزد
نابجایی گرم برخیزد
هوشمندی
سرد بنشیند

The dark path, an enemy of my feet.
At every moment dirty water and stones make for hardship.
But I walk the path using eyes as feet.

رهِ تاریک
با پاهای من پیکار دارد
به هر دم
زیرِ پایم راه را با آب آلوده
به سنگ آکنده و دشوار دارد؛
به چشمِ پا ولی
من راهِ خود را می سپارم

The wind, wandering.
Door open, light off.
Every house in the village is empty.
The one with a load on his shoulder, walking the path,
    over the bridge, is afraid.

باد می گردد و در باز و
چراغ است خموش
خانه ها یکسره خالی شده در دهکده اند
بیمناک است به ره
بار به دوشی که
به پل
راهِ خود می سپرد

I come from dust.
I love the sea.
In every direction my eyes see nothing but sea.
It steals my heart.
Where will my path reveal itself to me?

من خاکی نسبِ دریا دوست
که به چشمم ز همه سو دریاست،
و آنچه ام دل بستاند با اوست،
در کجا راهم روزی پیداست؟

My arrow falls to the ground.

هدفِ تیرِ من آید
در گِل

Your arrow finds the heart.

هدفِ تیرِ تو امّا
در دل

It is reward enough for you
    that not everyone knows your pain.

این تو را بس باشد،
که آشنای رنجت،
نه همه کس باشد

So long as the world moves, everyone is on his own path.

جهان تا جنبشی دارد
رَود هر کس
به راهِ خود

Morning light burns in the distance.
I think about it.
Come, companion, sing with me!

چراغ صبح می سوزد به راهِ دور
سوی او نظر با من
بخوان ای همسفر
با من!

From now on keep the door closed.
No one wants to meet anyone.

در فرو بند دگر
هیچ کسی
نیستش با کس
رایِ دیدار

The old hazelnut tree stands, casting shadows
    across the ground, where the creek stops flowing.
A branch withered, a leaf turned yellow.
The wind came and swept it all away.

در آن جایگه که
فندقِ پیر
سایه در سایه بر زمین گسترد
چون بماند آبِ جوی
از رفتار
شاخه ای خشک کرد و
برگی زرد
آمدش باد و با شتاب ببرد

Why is the door split and window broken?
Why is every room dark?
Why is it that a friend never asks about friends,
    about how they are?

از چیست در شکسته و
بگسسته پنجره؟
دیگر چرا که اتاقی
روشن نمی شود به چراغی؟
یک لحظه از رفیق رفیقی
جویا نمانده
نمی پرسد از
سرگذشته ای و سراغی؟

The heart should be the eye,
    able to find meaning in every colour.

چشم دل می باید
که ز هرِ رنگ
به معنی آید

The heart of the blossoming forest awakens.
The jasmine sleeps, soft in its embrace.

بیشه بشکفته به دل بیدار است
یاسمن خفته
در آغوشش نرم

Turn towards the valleys, asleep in mountain embrace,
    the shining dream of morning, towards everything
    barren or fertile, every open plain.
Call him!

بر سوی درّه ها
که در آغوشِ کوه ها
خواب و خیالِ روشنِ صبح اند
بر سوی هر خراب و هر آباد
هر دشت و هر دمن
او را صدا بزن!

It is up to us if something stays or goes.
Those who proclaim they want nothing
    are in truth avaricious.
The immobile long to fly.

لیک با ماست اگر می پاید
یا نمی پاید چیزی با ما
هیچ ناخواستن
از حرمتِ بس خواستن است،
بهرِ جنبیدن بسیارتری است
نه ز جا جنبیدن

Moonlight creeps through.
The glowworm shines.
Nothing can shatter anyone's sleep.
But thinking of them causes me to awaken with tearful eyes.

می تروادِ مهتاب
می درخشد شبتاب
نیست یک دم شکند
خواب به چشمِ کس و لیک
غمِ این خفتهٔ چند
خواب در چشمِ تَرَم می شکند

The names of certain people
    have become my soul's daily bread.
At moments of melancholy
    I stretch out my hands towards them.
They give me courage.
They empower me.

نامِ بعضی نفرات
رزقِ روحم شده است
وقتِ هرِ دلتنگی
سویشان دارم دست
جرأتم می بخشد
روشنم می دارد

All life's worries disappear in the middle of the night.

با دلِ شب
نه غم از بود و نبود

I have arrived from the desert with ravaged feet.

پای آبله
از راهِ بیابان رسیده ام

The creek weeps.
The moon laughs.
She laughs at my heart's desire.

جوی می گرید و
مه خندان است
و او به میلِ دلِ من
می خندد

Damn it all, including this and that letter of the alphabet,
 if I make mention of her.

لعنت به هر چه هست
از «تا» ز «خ» ز «میم»
از «شین»
گر اسم آورم از او

Ruins contain treasure.

گنج است
خراب را در آغوش!

Shining moon.
River calm.

ماه می‌تابد
رود است آرام

I stretch out my hands to open a door.
I am wasting my time.
Broken walls and doors collapse upon me.

دست ها می سایم
تا دری بگشایم
بی عبث می پایم
که به در کس آید
در و دیوارِ به هم ریخته شان
بر سرم می شکند

Be patient with me when fatigue overwhelms.
Open the door to dialogue.
But please, no blame or bitterness.

در موسمی که
خستگی ام می برد ز جای
با من بدار حوصله
بگشای در ز حرف
اما در آن نه ذرّه عتاب و
خطابِ تلخ!

A quiet forest path.
All that remains is a string of stones forming an oven,
    full of cold ashes, from nights long ago.

مانده از شب‌های دورِ دور
بر مسیرِ خامشِ جنگل
سنگچینی از اجاقی خرد
اندرو خاکسترِ سردی

Wind knocks and swipes at the frightened road.
A woman remains silent.

باد می‌کوبد
می‌روبد
جادّهٔ ترسان را
و زنی مانده خموش

Who remains?
Who is weary?

کیست کو مانده؟
کیست کو خسته است؟

Above the plain it rains a wonderful rain.

بر فرازِ دشت باران است
بارانِ عجیبی!

Beside the river rambles the old turtle.
Sunny day.

در کنار رودخانه می پلکد
سنگ پشتِ پیر
روز
روزِ آفتابی است

When will the iron melt in my hands?
When will I forge it?
Such stubborn iron.

کی به دستِ من
آهن من گرم خواهد شد
و من او را نرم خواهم ساخت؟
آهنِ سرسخت

I have no pain.
A stubborn fever has laid me low.
I know why the threads of my body feel stiff,
    as if at every moment each were lashing me
    from top to bottom.

من به تن دردم نیست
یک تب سرکش، تنها پکرم ساخته و دانم
این را که چرا
و چرا هر رگِ من در تنِ من
سفت و شلاقی است
که فرود آمده سوزان
دم به دم در تنِ من

I retain all suffering in my heart
    and all arrows of blame in my guts.
I long for that day when, picturing your face,
    I smile and ask of those travelling to the city,
    "What news of her?"

من همه رنج به دل می بندم
و همهِ تیرِ ملامت به جگر
به خیالی که می آید روزی
که به دیدار رُخَت می خندم
وز هرِ آنکس که برِ آن شهرِ سفر دارد
می پرسم:
«داری از او خبری؟»

A mercenary's work is best done for free.

خدمتی را که مزد
مزدوری است
خدمتِ ما به رایگان بهتر

It should be clear to you when I say that
many hands make light work.

مقصود من ز حرفم
معلوم بر شماست:
یک دست بی صداست

We have committed no crime, except to tread upon the path.

مرا گنهی نیست
به جز ره که نمودیم

My boat has run aground.
I am upset.

من چهره‌ام گرفته
من قایقم نشسته به خشکی

I am in pain.
From my pain spills blood.

من درد می بَرم
خون از درونِ دردم
سر ریز می کند

He hands over the keys of the locked locks
of the dirty rusty chain to be repaired.

او کلیدِ
قفل های بستهٔ زنجیرِ زنگ آلوده ای را
می دهد تعمیر

She who weeps when night is all around
    has a secret conversation with me.
She laughs with me.
She arrives laughing and laughing.

آن که می گرید با گردشِ شب
گفت و گو دارد با من به نهان
از برای من خندان است
آن که می آید
خندان، خندان

Such an honour to be free with life for a moment,
    to desire fearlessly, to talk about desiring fearlessly.
Such happiness!

چه بَرومندی
دمی با زندگی آزاد بودن
خواستن بی ترس
حرف از خواستن بی ترس گفتن
شاد بودن!

Silent is the man who each day peered through the window, awaiting a rainy night, like tonight.

هیچ آوایی نمی آید
از آن مردی که در آن پنجره
هر روز
چشم در راه شبی مانندِ امشب
بود بارانی

Everyone's spouse but mine has returned home.
My spouse is far away, working.

همسرِ هر کس
به خانه باز گردیده است
اِلّا همسرِ من
که ز من دور است و
در کار است

For some time now a bad feeling
    has been growing deep within.
My friends, my intimate friends!

پا گرفته است، زمانی است مدید
ناخوش احوالی
در پیکرِ من
دوستانم، رفقای محرم!

I am focused on my work, he is focused on me.
I seek a homeward path, he seeks a path to nowhere.

من در پیِ کار خود و
او در پیِ من
من راه به خانه خواهم
او راه برِ آب

My home is cloudy.
Clouds always hang heavy.

خانه ام ابری است
یکسره روی زمین
ابری است با آن

For a long time my neighbour's home has sat empty.

خالی افتاده است اما
خانهٔ همسایهٔ من
دیرگاهی است

The host sits alone at home.

میزبان
در خانه اش تنها نشسته

The sky rains down continuously upon the port.

آسمان یکریز می بارد
روی بندرگاه

I experienced the learning curve of youth.
My youthful days immersed in love as sweet as promises,
   but also bitter love.
Anyway, now my youth is behind me.

بودم به کارگاهِ جوانی
دورانِ روزهای جوانی مرا گذشت
در عشق های دلکش و شیرین
- شیرین چو وعده ها
یا عشق های تلخ کزِ آنم نبود
کام
فی الجمله گشت دورِ جوانی مرا
تمام

I am melancholic.
The guesthouse kills those who inhabit it.
I wish misfortune upon it.
Let its days be dark.
It has thrown together a crowd of people,
    some drowsy, some disagreeable, some absent-minded.

من دلم سخت گرفته است از این
میهمان خانهٔ مهمان کُشِ
روزش تاریک
که به جانِ هم نشناخته
انداخته است:
چند تن خواب آلود
چند تن ناهموار
چند تن ناهوشیار

Turbulent sea envelops impatient boatman.
Night, filled with danger, is frightening.

سخت طوفان زده روی دریاست
ناشکیباست به دل
قایق بان
شب پر از حادثه
دهشت افزاست

I have closed the door.
The night is upon me, my night, dark as the grave.
Although I am not that far from it, it is far from me.

در بسته‌ام، شب است
با من، شبِ من
تاریک همچو گور
با آنکه دور از او نه چنانم
او از من است دور

Night.
Valleys, still and sleeping, like dead snakes.
The hands of morning glory
    grasp the feet of the mountain cypress.
Whether or not you remember me,
    my memory of you remains strong.
My eyes upon the path, watching for you.

شباهنگام
در آن دم که برجا دره ها
چون مرده ماران خفتگانند؛
در آن نوبت که بندد دستِ نیلوفر
به پای سروِ کوهی دام
گَرَم یاد آوری یا نه
من از یادت نمی کاهم
تو را من چشم در راهم

A drought upon my farm, beside my neighbour's farm.
"They weep upon the nearby seashore," we are told.
    "Mourner upon mourner."
Tell me, messenger of cloudy days, you tree frog,
    when do the rains arrive?

خشک آمد کشتگاهِ من
در جوارِ کشتِ همسایه
گر چه می گویند:
«می گریند روی ساحلِ نزدیک
سوگواران در میانِ سوگواران.»
قاصدِ روزانِ ابری
داروگ!
کی می رسد باران؟

Spread across the floor are all my unwanted things.
In my darkened hut there can be no joy.
The walls of bamboo, dry as dust, about to explode,
    like hearts of lovers separated.
Tell me, messenger of cloudy days, you tree frog,
    when do the rains arrive?

بر بساطی که
بساطی نیست
در درونِ کومهٔ تاریکِ من
که ذرّه ای با آن نشاطی نیست
و جدارِ دنده های نی
به دیوارِ اتاقم
دارد از خشکیش می تَرَکد
ـ چون دلِ یاران که در هجرانِ یاران ـ
قاصدِ روزانِ ابری
داروگ!
کی می رسد باران؟

At every moment is the white flower, like a beautiful face,
	smiling.
It tells a myth to the night.
The bird of happiness, anguished, shaken with suffering,
	talks nonstop.
It spreads a wing, the colour of blood,
	then sits, unhappy, on an overturned stone.

هر دم گلِ سفید
که مانند روی گل
بگشاده است روی
با شب فسانه گوست
مرغ طرب، فتاده به تشویش
با رنج های دگرگون
هر دم به گفت وگوست
او باز می کند بالی
به رنگِ خون
و افسرده می نشیند
برِ سنگِ واژگون

But the road is empty of everyone.
Debris upon debris.

جادّه امّا ز همه کس خالی است
ریخته بر سرِ آوار، آوار

The unawakened have many worries, but for no good reason.

خفته هزار غم خورد
از بهر هیچ چیز

Poetry is a sign of our desert dream.

شعر
آیتی از خیالِ صحراییِ ماست

Unlike all others, my ears are my eyes.

تنها منم آن که گوشِ من
چشمِ من است

I do not listen to words of hypocrisy.

گوشم
نه به حرفِ هرِ ریایی باشد

We are hanged by a hair.

ما را
به یکی موی، بیاویخته اند

O God!
Contemplation of those blue eyes.

آوخ ز نگه کردنِ آن
چشم کبود

My heart wanders because of your love.

سرگشته دلم
که اندرو، مهرِ تو بود

With poverty comes one thousand wrongdoings.

با تهی کیسگی
هزار خطاست

Nothing has gone as I had hoped.
Meaninglessly, I continue chasing my dreams.

بر مرادم نمی رود کاری
به عبث مانده ام مریدِ مراد

I am the poet of another people.
Among all others, I am the other.

من شاعرِ مردمی دگر هستم
وز بینِ همه دگر،
دگرسانم.

Friends who travelled together have all left the festivities.
Grieving for them is the best thing to do.

گشت مجلس تهی
ز هم سفران
غمِ یارانِ مهربان بهتر

A free man accepts no chains.

مردی که رهاست
قید نپذیرد

Shoes over here, feet over there.

کفش سویی بمانده
پا سویی.

Destroy timeworn foundations.
Today I sing alone.

ویران کن هر اساسِ فرسوده
امروز منم که فرد می خوانم

I would rather be mute than a famous speaker.

گر لال شود زبانِ من، بهتر
تا شهره شوم که من سخن دانم

Better than any words are those of the heart.

حرفِ دل
بهتر از هر حرفی است

Published by Sticking Place Books

Lessons with Kiarostami
Edited by Paul Cronin

A Wolf on Watch (dual-language)
Poems by Abbas Kiarostami

With the Wind (dual-language)
Poems by Abbas Kiarostami

Wind and Leaf (dual-language)
Poems by Abbas Kiarostami

Wine (dual-language)
Poetry by Hafez
Selected and adapted by Abbas Kiarostami

Tears (two volumes) (dual-language)
Poetry by Saadi
Selected and adapted by Abbas Kiarostami

Water (dual-language)
Poetry by Nima
Selected and adapted by Abbas Kiarostami

Fire (four volumes) (dual-language)
Poetry by Rumi
Selected and adapted by Abbas Kiarostami

Night (two volumes) (dual-language)
Poetry from the Classical Persian Canon
Selected and adapted by Abbas Kiarostami

Night (two volumes) (dual-language)
Poetry from the Contemporary Persian Canon
Selected and adapted by Abbas Kiarostami

In the Shadow of Trees
The Collected Poetry of Abbas Kiarostami

www.ingramcontent.com/pod-product-compliance
Lightning Source LLC
Chambersburg PA
CBHW042233090526
44588CB00005B/69